You're ROAR some !!!

...

Prof. Ben

ULTIMATE DINOSAURS

SPINOSAURUS

BEN GARROD

ULTIMATE DINOSAURS
SPINOSAURUS

ZEPHYR

An imprint of Head of Zeus

First published in the UK in 2018 by Zephyr, an imprint of Head of Zeus
This revised and updated Zephyr paperback edition first published in the UK
in 2023 by Head of Zeus, part of Bloomsbury Publishing Plc

Text © Ben Garrod, 2023

Palaeo Art © Scott Hartman, 2023, and Gabriel Ugueto, 2023

Cartoon illustrations © Ethan Kocak, 2023

9 8 7 6 5 4 3 2 1

A CIP catalogue record for this book is available from the British Library.

ISBN (PB): 9781804549674
ISBN (E): 9781035902965

Designed by Nicky Borowiec

Printed and bound in Great Britain
by CPI Group (UK) Ltd, Croydon CR0 4YY

MIX
Paper | Supporting
responsible forestry
FSC
www.fsc.org
FSC® C171272

Head of Zeus
5–8 Hardwick Street
London EC1R 4RG

WWW.HEADOFZEUS.COM

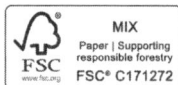

For geeky scientists

who are super-heroes too

CONTENTS

I was born loving animals. I used to watch birds and squirrels and frogs in our garden and on the cliffs above the sea. When I was ten years old, I decided I would go to Africa, live with wild animals and write books about them. Everyone laughed – Africa was far away – and I was just a girl. Back then (1944), girls didn't get to do things like that. But my mother said, 'If you really want this you must work hard, take advantage of opportunities, and *never give up.*' That is the message I have for you.

My dream came true when I met Dr Louis Leakey and was able to study chimpanzees in Gombe National Park, Tanzania. Chimpanzees helped me prove to science that like humans, animals have personalities, minds and emotions. Eventually I built a research station and my students are *still* learning new things about the Gombe chimpanzees. Just as scientists are always learning about new species of dinosaur.

8

INTRODUCTION

by JANE GOODALL, PhD, DBE

Founder - the Jane Goodall
Institute & UN Messenger of Peace

I have known Prof Ben for years and he and I both encourage you to follow *your* dreams. Maybe you don't plan to be a scientist, but even so you need to learn about the work scientists do, for it helps us understand so much about the wonderful world we live in – about evolution and the incredible variety of species. And there are many more species not yet discovered. Maybe you will discover one of them! Maybe it will be named after you!

Whatever you decide to do, I hope you'll always be curious about our magical world and inspired by the people who spend their lives uncovering her secrets and sharing them. And, above all, that you will join Prof Ben and me in our efforts to conserve life on planet Earth.

HEY EVERYONE!

Growing up isn't always easy, particularly if you're the only one in your family picking up dead sharks from the beach, learning to dissect animals when you're ten, or trying to catch snakes with a broom. And yes, I did all of those (and trying to catch snakes was not my best idea, so please don't do it), but it's worse if you're the only one in your school doing these things. It's easier to try to blend with the crowd, so that no one picks on you or because you don't want to be thought of as weird. **But remember there are *always* other wonderful weird people out there**, who know exactly what you're going through and they're there to help encourage and support you.

Whether it's at your local museum, geology society, wildlife club, or at school, Scouts, Guides, or with your family or friends, **never feel that you can't talk to others who share your interests**. Of course, I have to remind you not to talk to strangers but, with the help of your parents or teachers, you'll find some science friends.

Some of the most inspirational geeks I know are young people who go bird watching every weekend or take amazing wildlife photos in all weathers. Some collect skulls they find on walks, others write blogs and articles about how young people (like you) have the power to change the world.

I know that many of these amazing young scientists have found things easier because they have others around them to chat to, discuss their passion with and to ask for advice about where the best fossils are, what a baby crow eats or how to bury a whale. Yes, I asked these things when I was a lot, lot younger.

I guess I'm saying two things here. **First, it's not always easy to be geeky but it helps to have other geeky people around you.** Being geeky just means you really love one thing, more than most people would. For example, I love science – I'm a science geek, my brother loves cars – he's a car geek. The second is that we should all be proud to be geeky. Let's make it your greatest strength. I have lived and worked all over the world, I've studied chimpanzees and sharks and I've been to the Arctic and to deserts. I have helped save rare species, been chased by hungry predators and I've filmed wild animals. I do research, teach at a university and make cool science programmes for TV. And, I'm a geek! Remember, be different, be weird, be geeky.

Now I'm a scientist, I would like to think that my students and the countless young people I meet can always talk to me about science, about being a young scientist and how much fun they're having. Besides, I always like to learn about new fossil sites, what a baby crow likes for breakfast and new ways to bury a whale. **By being you, you will be the best type of scientist you can be . . . you'll be a happy scientist.**

Let's get geeky!

Ben

If you have been wondering who I am as you've been reading the *Ultimate Dinosaurs* series, then it's about time we were introduced. I'm *Epidexipteryx* (*eppi-dex ip-terr-iks*) or 'display feather'. Only one fossil of me has been found so far and that was in Mongolia from around 160 million years ago.

With a 25cm-long skeleton, I was one of the smallest dinosaurs and I was pretty weird. I had large eyes, huge claws and spindly little teeth at the front of my mouth, which was really unusual in theropods. I also had four long tail feathers, which I most likely used for display. I was the first dinosaur to use feathers for showing off.

CHAPTER 1

DINOSAUR DEFINITIONS

WHAT *IS* A DINOSAUR?

YOU'RE DEFINITELY NOT FAMILY!

I love dinosaurs, you love dinosaurs, we all love dinosaurs. It's not a huge surprise that they are popular. They're just so cool. But when did that palaeo passion start? Who were the first palaeontologists and dino-discoverers? Way, way back in the past, people had no idea what dinosaurs (or even fossils) were. When some fossil bones were found in a cave in Italy, people thought that because they were so big, the bones must have belonged to giant humans. Okay, stop laughing, it made sense at the time. They thought these giants were over 90m tall, almost as long as *three* diplodocuses. Now you can laugh. It is said even the ancient Greeks thought the fossil skulls of small island-living elephants belonged to giant ogres called Cyclops, and that the hole in the skull for the nostrils and trunk was actually for their single big eye. Have a look at an elephant skull the next time you're in a museum and see if you can imagine it as a one-eyed giant's skull.

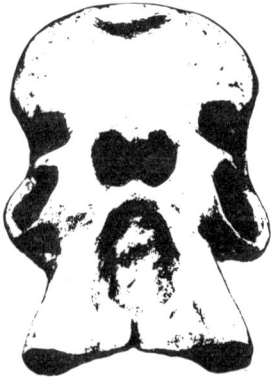

Remember, science isn't just about discoveries and facts. It's also about the people who make those discoveries and who are responsible for the new ways we look at the world around us. So, who were some of the most important and most interesting early palaeontologists and fossil hunters?

One of the most important people in our understanding of dinosaurs early on was **William Buckland**. He was a geologist (which means he loved studying rocks) and a palaeontologist. He was also the first person to write about dinosaurs in a proper scientific way and, in 1824, was the first to name *Megalosaurus*, which was found in Oxford, UK. At this time, the word 'dinosaur' had never been used. Before he named *Megalosaurus*, other people had thought that the bones were either from a war elephant brought over by the Romans or from a giant from the Bible. As if being the first person to describe a dinosaur wasn't enough, he was also fascinated by poo. Not just any poo but fossilised poo . . . or 'coprolites' as they're called (he was the first to use the word coprolite too).

William Buckland wasn't the first to discover coprolites though. A famous fossil hunter called **Mary Anning** was already interested in them. Mary grew up in a village called Lyme Regis, on the southern coast of the UK. Where did she find these fossilised poos? She found them inside the remains of ichthyosaur skeletons. Mary found the first ichthyosaur skeleton that was correctly identified (before that, people thought they were some weird crocodile sort of thing). She also found some of the very first plesiosaur and pterosaur fossils. Mary was one of the most important people in helping the world understand prehistoric animals and what life used to be like on Earth. Now, we all know how important Mary is to science, but back then it was almost impossible for girls or women to be in science. They could not vote or go to university or join scientific societies. Because of this, men claimed a lot of Mary's ideas and discoveries, which was really unfair. Luckily, girls play a big part in science now and Mary is definitely a great role model for all of us.

You may have heard of **Richard Owen**. He is one of *the* best-known palaeontologists ever. His two greatest achievements were first, being a major reason why the London Natural History Museum was built and looks the way it does (which is pretty cool), and second, for actually making up the word 'dinosaur' (which is *really* cool). Seems like a good guy, hey? Well, he was and he wasn't . . . he did lots of great things that many young scientists should look up to, but he also did a few unwise things. I'm not going to say he stole ideas but there were definitely times he said, 'Wow, look what I've found' when he hadn't made the discovery. He told the world that he discovered *Iguanodon* . . . when the truth is another palaeontologist called **Gideon Mantell** actually found it. Awkward! Richard Owen is a lesson to us all . . . you can be great in science if you discover awesome things, but if you can't get on with people and behave badly, then you'll be remembered for that.

As you've seen, the science of dinosaurs and other extinct species is often based on the work of the great fossil hunters and palaeontologists who were around in the early years of the study. The way these people thought, the things they found and the methods they used to understand fossil finds, still help us today. Sometimes, though, these palaeo pioneers acted in a way that may seem a little strange.

The best example of this is the **Bone Wars**. Two *friendly* palaeontologists in the United States (**Edward Drinker Cope** and **Othniel Charles Marsh**) fell out when they started discovering amazing fossils and lots of new species of dinosaurs. Rather than working together as a team, they did some terrible things. It's hard to know for sure who started what, but they seem to have been as bad as each other. They attempted to ruin each other's reputation and tried to make sure money to fund the other's fossil digs was taken away. They stole fossils from one another and even used dynamite to destroy fossils in the ground so that the other couldn't get them. Unbelievable, hey! When Cope made a rather silly mistake by putting the skull on the tail (rather than the neck) of a new pliosaur species, Marsh made sure everyone found out. It might sound funny, but this isn't the way you'd imagine scientists would behave, is it? Marsh made a similar mistake when he put the wrong skull on the

EDWARD DRINKER COPE

OTHNIEL CHARLES MARSH

DIPLODOCUS SKULL

body of a sauropod skeleton. And on and on it went, but between them, they discovered over 120 new prehistoric species.

It was palaeontologists and fossil hunters like these who helped us realise that not only were the dinosaurs very different to other animals but they were also an entirely different group.

It's easy to think that these early palaeo heroes got it all sorted. Okay, maybe you're thinking, 'Hang on Ben, they didn't have lasers and scanners and computers and having these things now means we need them to fully understand dinosaurs.' Well, neither is true. Yes, those science pioneers *did* clear the path for us and we learned so much from them. The use of modern technology *has* helped us loads, but the truth is that there is still so, so much we have to discover and learn about dinosaurs.

DEFINITELY DINOSAURS

It may seem odd but we don't have an exact definition of what a dinosaur is. This is because there were so many different types. Some were small, some were huge.

Some had two legs, some had four. Some were hunters and others were herbivores. With so many differences, it makes it hard to have a set of rules that works for every fossil. Instead, we use rough guidelines – if a fossil has most of the following, then scientists can be pretty certain they're dealing with a dinosaur.

1. **Dinosaurs have two holes behind each eye towards the back of the skull.** This means they are diapsids. If you're wondering, we (as mammals) belong to the synapsid group, all of which have only one hole behind each eye. When you're in your local museum, look at any dinosaur skeleton. The skull should have two holes just behind the eye.

2. **Dinosaurs all have straight legs.** Next time you see a crocodile when you're out for a walk, have a look at its legs (just don't get too close). Rather than legs that stand straight like ours, their legs bend out in the middle somewhere. All reptiles with legs, such as crocs and their relatives and many lizards, have legs that look the same – they come out from the body to the side and then go down.

CROCODILE

All dinosaurs (whether with four legs or two) walked with their legs held in a straight line beneath their body. This meant dinosaurs could breathe easily as they walked or ran – great for chasing other dinosaurs, or running away from them. It also allowed them to become much bigger than if they had legs with a bend in the middle.

DINOSAUR

3. Dinosaurs have short arms. We all know that *Tyrannosaurus rex* and its relatives had teeny arms, but almost every dinosaur had forelimbs slightly shorter than you might expect. Have a look at your arms – the upper arm bone (humerus) is only a little longer than the two lower arm bones (radius and ulna). In dinosaurs, the radius is nearly always at least 20 per cent shorter than the humerus.

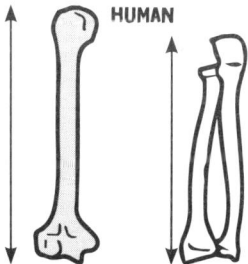

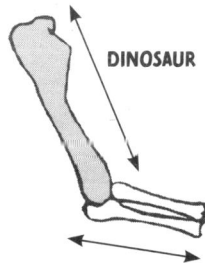

HUMAN

DINOSAUR

DINO CHECKLIST

Between the two holes behind the eye, there is a dimple (called a **fossa**) in the bone.

Most of the neck bones (**vertebrae**) have extra bits of bone that look like a little diagonally backwards-facing wing on each side. These are called '**epipophyses**' (*eppi-pofe ee-sees*).

There is a ridge along the edge of the **humerus** for big muscles to attach to. In dinosaurs, this ridge is more than 30 per cent of the way along the bone.

The ridge (called the **fourth trochanter**) on the **femur** (thigh bone), which the leg muscles attach to, is strong and looks 'sharp'.

The bones at the back of the **skull** do not meet in the middle.

The ridge on the **tibia** (shin bone) curves to the front and outwards.

At the place where the **fibula** (one of the lower leg bones) joins the ankle, there's a dip on the ankle bone.

CHAPTER 2

DINOSAUR DETECTIVES

Spinosaurus

There's one dinosaur that is the most mysterious, is the cause of more debate than any other and poses many questions we still need to answer. That tricky predatory dinosaur is *Spinosaurus*.

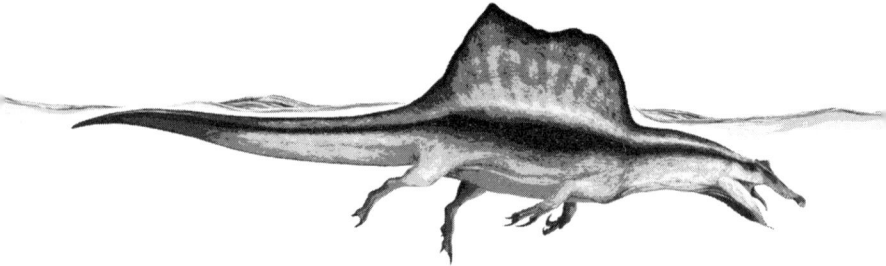

The first fossils were found in Egypt in 1912 by a palaeontologist from Germany, called Ernst Stromer. They included vertebrae, a huge lower jaw, teeth and a few of the long spines that have made this species so famous. Stromer did everything a good scientist should have done. He described the fossils, took photographs and drew them in perfect detail. This was really useful, as a bomb was dropped on the museum that housed the *Spinosaurus* fossils in 1944, destroying them forever. Since then, more fossils have been found but not enough for us to understand *Spinosaurus*.

The name *Spinosaurus* is made up from two words, 'spino-' meaning *spine* and '-saurus' meaning *lizard* and so far, we're sure there was definitely one species, *Spinosaurus aegyptiacus* (spine lizard from Egypt). But perhaps there was a second species, *Spinosaurus maroccanus* (spine lizard from Morocco). Scientists don't have enough information to be certain either way, yet.

This was one of the largest theropod dinosaurs ever, maybe the biggest. *Spinosaurus* was roughly the same size as massive killers such as *Giganotosaurus*, *Carcharodontosaurus* and possibly *Tyrannosaurus rex*. *Spinosaurus* was alive in the mid-Cretaceous period, between 112–93.5 million years ago.

These huge predators weighed somewhere between 7 and 20 tonnes (in fact, there's nothing that walks on land that is this big – *Spinosaurus* weighed as much as three killer whales) and would have measured up

to 18m long. Not only was *Spinosaurus* a super-sized dinosaur but it also looked different. It had a long skull with a thin snout and lots of slender teeth with sharp tips. Some scientists think it walked on its two longer back legs (although there's an argument over that which I'll talk about later), but it was the row of long spines running the length of its back, which made this a truly distinctive dinosaur. Some of these bony spines were up to 1.65m in length (as tall as an adult human) and there was probably skin between the spines, making one big sail. But exactly what this sail was used for was a very different matter and we'll come to that later.

FAMILY TREE

Spinosaurus was the biggest of a group of theropod dinosaurs called the spinosaurs. It was a predatory dinosaur with a long skull, similar to crocodiles. It had cone-shaped teeth that had few (or no) serrations. If you look at the skull from above, the snout ends in a rounded tip, with lots of teeth, called a rosette. This is seen in all the spinosaurs and helps palaeontologists to identify them. Fossils from spinosaurs have been found in Africa, Europe, South America and Asia.

The spinosaurs belonged to a family called Spinosauridae. These dinosaurs belong with the Megalosauridea dinosaurs in a bigger group, meaning spinosaurs such as *Spinosaurus* were most closely related to other theropod dinosaurs such as *Megalosaurus*.

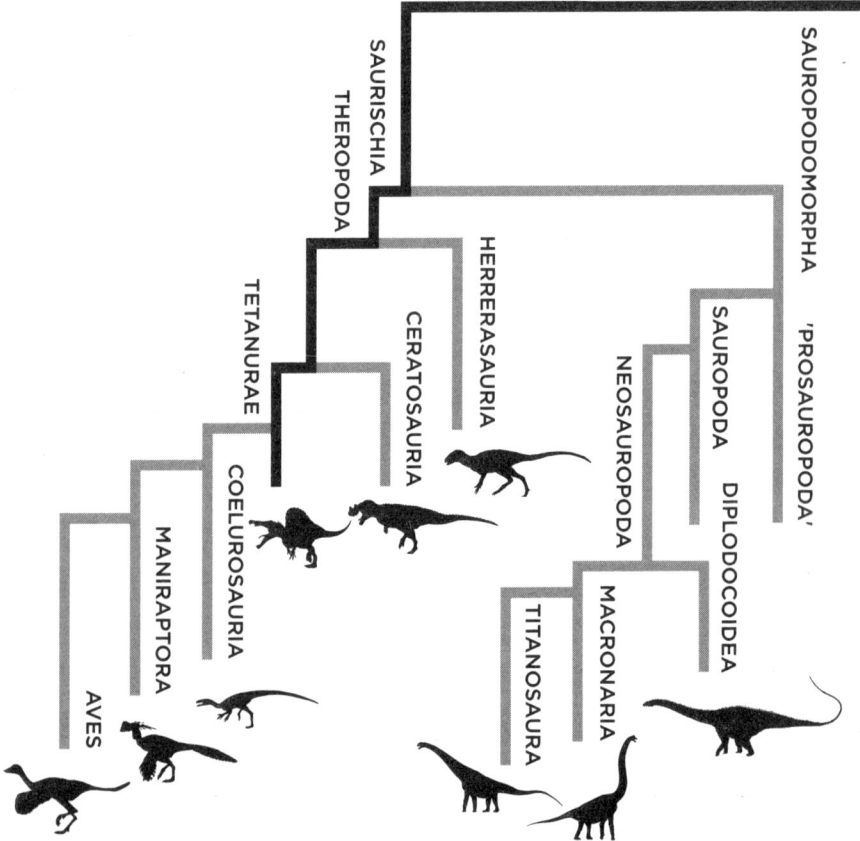

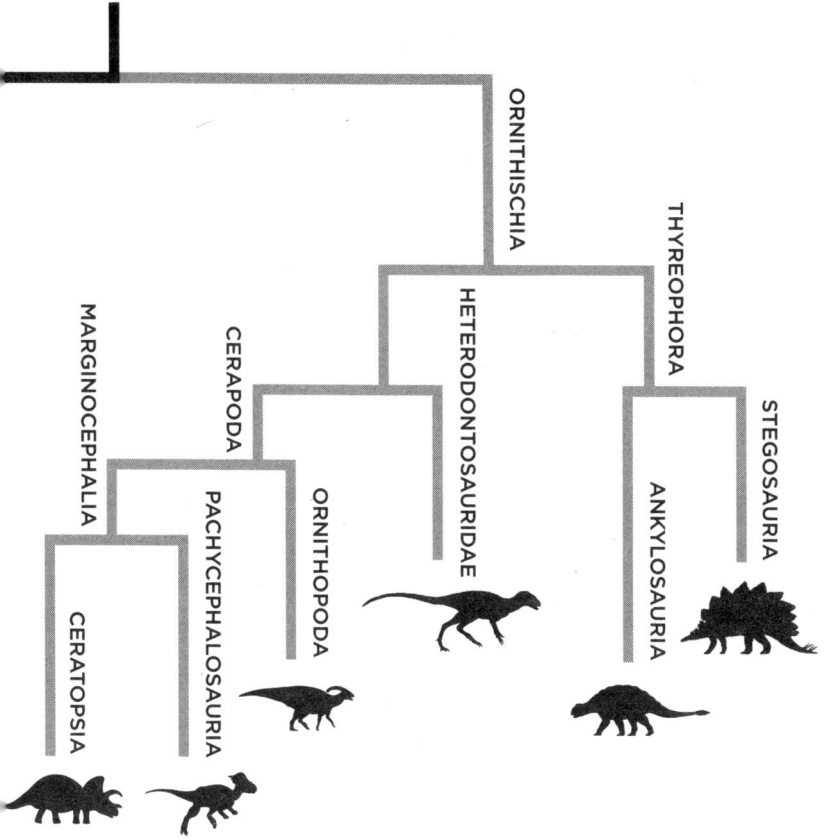

DINOSAURIA

ORNITHISCHIA

THYREOPHORA

MARGINOCEPHALIA

CERAPODA

HETERODONTOSAURIDAE

STEGOSAURIA

PACHYCEPHALOSAURIA

ORNITHOPODA

ANKYLOSAURIA

CERATOPSIA

SPINOSAURIDAE

Spinosaurinae

Baryonychinae

The Spinosauridae group sits on the Tetanurae branch of the more complete dinosaur family tree. Look closely at the Spinosauridae and you'll see there are two main branches in this family, the Baryonychinae and Spinosaurinae. In the first group are *Suchomimus* from Niger in central Africa, *Ichthyovenator* from Laos and *Baryonyx* from southern England. Both *Spinosaurus* from Africa and *Irritator* from Brazil are included in the other group, Spinosaurinae, meaning *Irritator* and *Spinosaurus* were most closely related.

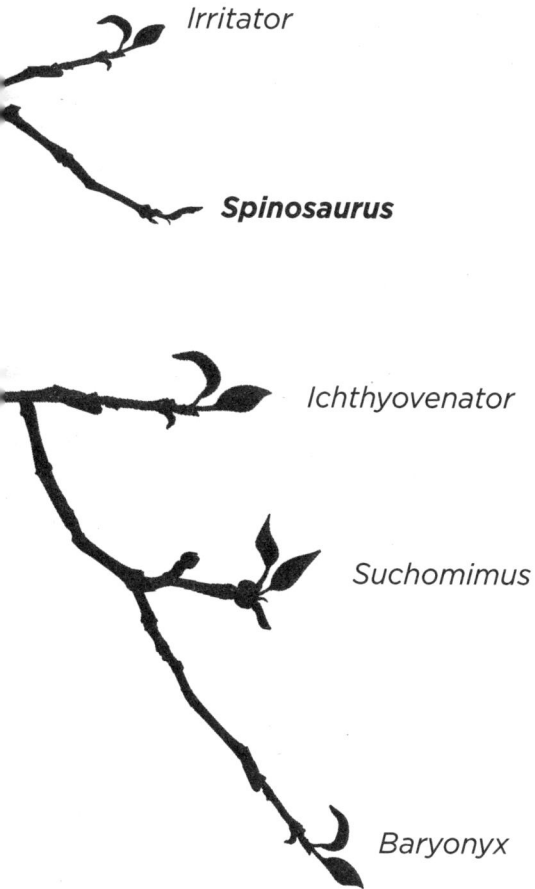

Irritator

Spinosaurus

Ichthyovenator

Suchomimus

Baryonyx

SPINOSAURUS RELATIVES

Irritator (*Ir-ree tay-tor*) 'irritating'

7.5m

This spinosaur was found in Brazil, South America. It was about 7.5m long and weighed around a tonne. It lived about 110 million years ago, in the Early Cretaceous. It had a crest at the back of the head and, like other spinosaurs, would have eaten fish. An *Irritator* tooth has been found embedded in the neck vertebrae of a pterosaur, but we are not sure if the dinosaur hunted or scavenged these hunting reptiles.

The only significant *Irritator* fossil found so far is a skull. Realising it was possibly from a new species, the palaeontologists bought it from some collectors who were trying to sell it illegally. To make it look more complete (and more expensive), the fossil collectors had added a load of clay and plaster. When they realised this, the palaeontologists were annoyed. They were so irritated that they called this new spinosaur, *Irritator*.

Ichthyovenator (*Ick-thee-o ven-ay-tor*) 'fish hunter'

9m

This was one of only two types of spinosaur to be discovered in Asia and fossils have only been found in Laos. It was 7.5–9m long and weighed about 1.5 tonnes. It would have lived during the Early Cretaceous, 125–113 million years ago.

So far, all we know about *Ichthyovenator* comes from one fossil find, in which nine vertebrae, parts of the pelvis and a rib were discovered. Although we don't yet have a skull, the discovery did tell the scientists something special about *Ichthyovenator*. Because so many vertebrae were found, it showed that this spinosaur had at least two separate sails running down its back.

Suchomimus (*Soo-ko my-muss*) 'crocodile mimic'

9m

This was an African spinosaur and fossils have been found in Niger. It was about 9m long and weighed approximately 2 tonnes. It would have lived about 125–112 million years ago in the Early Cretaceous. The main fossil specimen from which we know most about *Suchomimus* was from a subadult animal, meaning it would not have been fully grown.

Suchomimus is a good reminder about how closely we need to look at fossils if we want to identify differences between species. Not only are there often only small differences between species' skeletons but also not many fossils of this dinosaur have been discovered so far. However, there are some things on the bones, such as an extra little arch in one of the bones in the snout, some slightly larger tail vertebrae, and a small hook-shaped piece of bone on the upper arm bone (the humerus), which show us this was a separate species.

Baryonyx (*Ba-ree on-ix*) 'heavy claw'

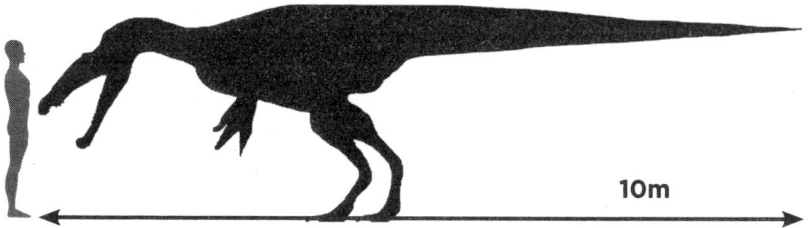

10m

This was a British spinosaur but fossils have also been found in Spain. It was 7–10m long and weighed 1–1.5 tonnes. It would have lived about 130–125 million years ago in the Early Cretaceous. It had a very large claw (about 30cm long) on the first finger on each forelimb, and a long narrow snout and jaws, which looked similar to those of a gharial crocodile from India. It also had a triangle-shaped crest at the top of the snout.

The first fossil found of *Baryonyx* is one of the best and most complete theropod fossils in the UK. It was the first predatory dinosaur that was shown to prey on fish – fish scales were found in the area where the stomach would have been on the fossil. Remains of a young *Iguanodon* were also found, but we don't know if this means *Baryonyx* was a predator or scavenger of other dinosaurs.

TEST YOUR DINO KNOWLEDGE HERE!

Who was the first person to identify an ichthyosaur skeleton?

Which word is Richard Owen famous for making up?

When was *Spinosaurus* alive?

Which modern reptile does *Spinosaurus* look similar to?

What special discoveries have scientists made from *Ichthyoventor* fossils?

All the answers are in the text and at the back of the book.

CHAPTER 3

DINOSAUR DISCOVERIES

WHEN AND WHERE

WHEN AND WHERE

The times when the dinosaurs existed can be split into three main chunks (what we call 'periods') and these are the **Triassic period**, the **Jurassic period** and the **Cretaceous period**. *Spinosaurus* was around in the middle of the Cretaceous, 112–93.5 million years ago. Fossils have been found across northern Africa, in both Morocco and Egypt.

During the Cretaceous, there were more types of dinosaur than at any other time and there were lots and lots of different types of predatory theropod dinosaur. The spinosaur family was found across much of the world, when the Earth looked very different to the way it does today.

During the early time of the dinosaurs, most of the land on Earth formed a huge supercontinent called Pangaea. This huge landmass began breaking up during the Jurassic but by the Cretaceous, it had started to divide into two major sections, Gondwana in the south and Laurasia in the north. *Spinosaurus* was found at the very northern edge of Gondwana. It seems that the spinosaurs evolved when Pangaea was a single landmass

THE WORLD IN THE MIDDLE CRETACEOUS PERIOD

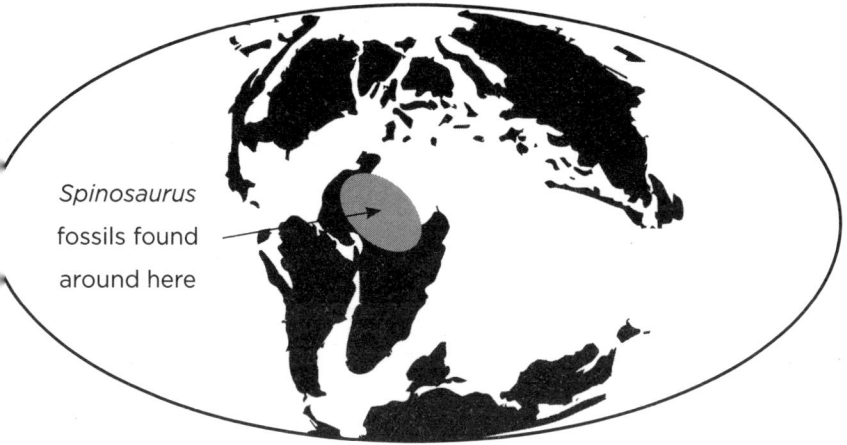

Spinosaurus fossils found around here

and that when these super-islands formed, the separate species such as *Irritator*, *Suchomimus* and *Spinosaurus* evolved separately.

Spinosaurus lived and hunted in and around the warm shores of lakes, rivers and tidal flats in North Africa during the Cretaceous. There was a large prehistoric sea in northeastern Africa back then, with lots of mangrove swamps in the area. It was hot and humid and changed from season to season, across the year. In the dry season, many of the lakes and rivers may have dried up, making hunting harder for predators such as *Spinosaurus*.

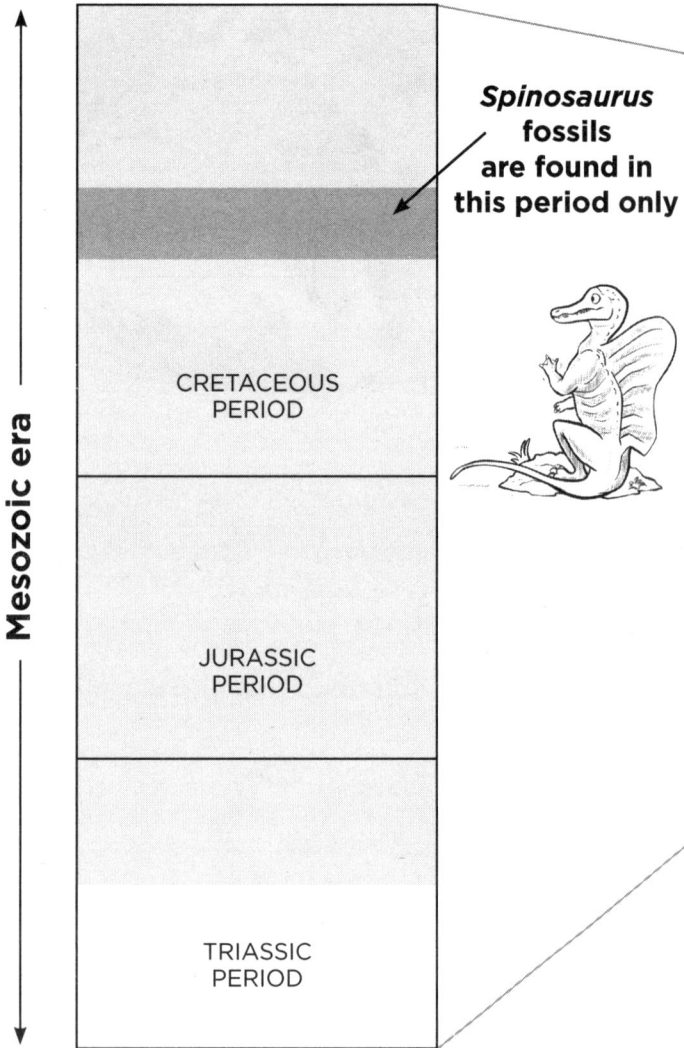

Mesozoic era

***Spinosaurus* fossils are found in this period only**

CRETACEOUS PERIOD

JURASSIC PERIOD

TRIASSIC PERIOD

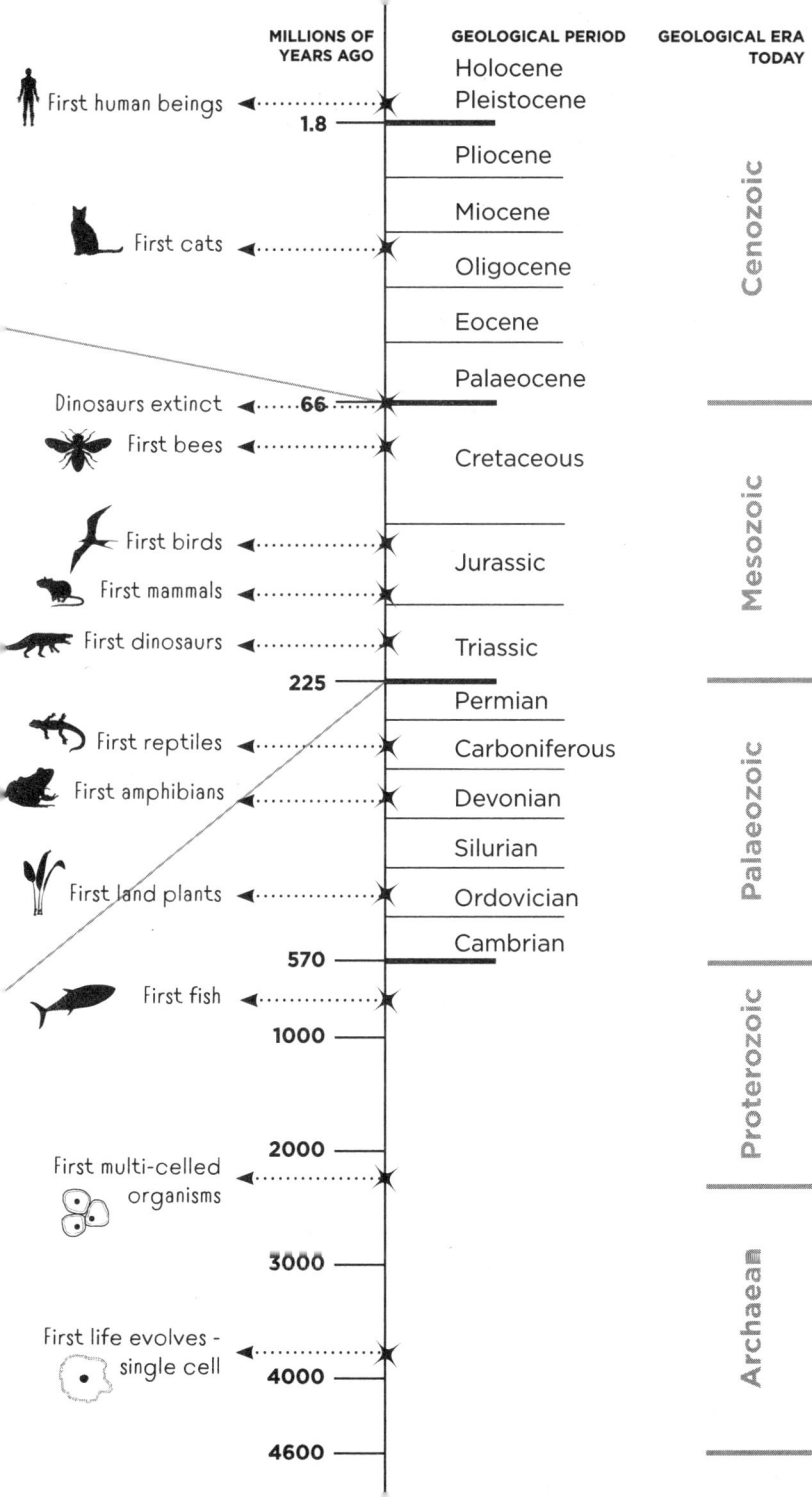

MILLIONS OF YEARS AGO	GEOLOGICAL PERIOD	GEOLOGICAL ERA TODAY
	Holocene	
First human beings ◄······· ✕	Pleistocene	
1.8 ─		
	Pliocene	Cenozoic
	Miocene	
First cats ◄·········· ✕	Oligocene	
	Eocene	
	Palaeocene	
Dinosaurs extinct ◄···**66**···✕		
First bees ◄··········· ✕	Cretaceous	
First birds ◄········· ✕		Mesozoic
First mammals ◄········· ✕	Jurassic	
First dinosaurs ◄·········· ✕	Triassic	
225 ─	Permian	
First reptiles ◄········· ✕	Carboniferous	
First amphibians ◄········· ✕	Devonian	Palaeozoic
	Silurian	
First land plants ◄·········· ✕	Ordovician	
570 ─	Cambrian	
First fish ◄·········· ✕		
1000 ─		Proterozoic
2000 ─		
First multi-celled organisms ◄········· ✕		
3000 ─		
First life evolves - single cell ◄········· ✕		Archaean
4000 ─		
4600 ─		

When *Spinosaurus* lived in North Africa, it was a weird watery world different from how it is today. But *Spinosaurus* wasn't the only big predator there - it shared its habitat with the giant crocodile *Sarcosuchus*. This super-croc would have been up to 12m long and weighed around 8 tonnes (a lot bigger than any croc alive today). We have no idea if these two huge predators ever met, but it seems very likely they must have occasionally bumped into each other. Did they fight? Did they even hunt each other? We may never know but it would have been fascinating to see.

WHAT HAPPENED TO THE DINOSAURS?

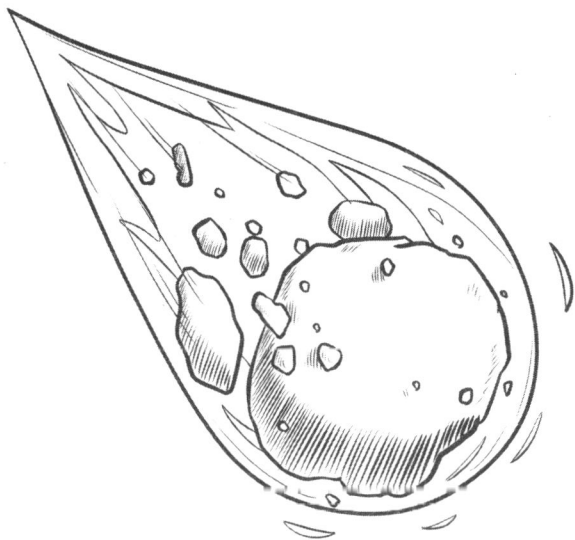

So many people work with dinosaurs –
from amateur collectors to world-famous scientists.
Some go looking for fossils in the ground, others study
them in laboratories and some recreate them
as incredible pieces of artwork.

DR STEVE BRUSATTE

Palaeontologist

University of Edinburgh,
Scotland (UK)

Dr Steve Brusatte works at the University of Edinburgh
in Scotland and specialises in the anatomy and
evolution of dinosaurs.

We asked Steve the following question:

'What actually happened to the dinosaurs?'

And this is what he told us:

'Ever since the first dinosaur bones were discovered many centuries ago, people have asked: why aren't these animals alive anymore? Dinosaurs ruled the world for over 150 million years during the Mesozoic Era, but there's nothing alive today that looks like a *T. rex* or a *Brontosaurus*.

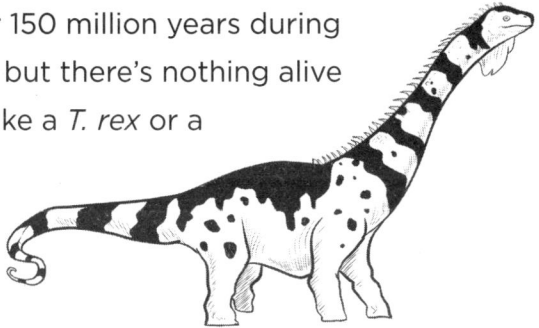

So what happened? Palaeontologists have come up with many theories about why the dinosaurs died out. Maybe they were unable to cope with changes in climate or temperature, and slowly disappeared. Maybe there was a sudden catastrophe, like a huge volcanic eruption or a massive flood that wiped them out in an instant. Or, maybe something even crazier occurred, like a virus or some type of genetic mutation.

Many of these theories are just guesses. But in the 1970s scientists finally started to collect enough evidence from fossils to understand why dinosaurs went extinct. Palaeontologists realised that dinosaurs disappeared all over the world at the same time, about 66 million years ago, at the end of the Cretaceous period. Many other animals died at this moment too: the flying pterosaurs, big reptiles in the oceans like mosasaurs and plesiosaurs, the shelled ammonites, and many thousands of other species. Something must have killed all these animals at once. But what?

A geologist named Walter Alvarez figured it out. He was in Italy studying rocks that were formed right at the end of the Cretaceous period. Walter tested the chemical composition of the rocks and noticed that they were full of a strange element called iridium. You have probably never heard of iridium, because it is very rare on Earth. But it is very common in outer space. Walter had an idea: maybe an asteroid came down from the heavens 66 million years ago, killing the dinosaurs.

He was proved right
when another team of
geologists found
a huge crater in Mexico,
which was made at the end
of the Cretaceous.

Imagine yourself in the scaly feet of a
T. rex that was alive 66 million years ago, in the forests
of North America. Everything seems peaceful and calm.
But then, up in the sky, a fireball appears. It gets closer
and closer, until it smashes into the Earth, unleashing
earthquakes, tidal waves, and fires. This was a bad time
to be alive. It was probably one of the worst days in the
history of Earth. T. rex couldn't deal with these sudden
catastrophes, and it died. And so did all of the other
dinosaurs.

Well, not ALL dinosaurs. One peculiar type of dinosaur did survive the asteroid impact: small, fast-growing, big-brained, meat-eating theropods with feathers and wings. Birds. Birds evolved from small theropod dinosaurs, which means birds are dinosaurs! When all of the other dinosaurs died, birds were able to fly away from the chaos of the asteroid. And they remain today, as over 10,000 species of modern-day dinosaurs!'

CHAPTER 4

DELVE INTO A DINOSAUR

ANATOMY OF A *SPINOSAURUS*

I'M OFF FOR A SWIM.

THE BONES

We know that *Spinosaurus* was one of the biggest of the predatory dinosaurs and one of the largest land predators of all time, but because we only have the skeletons, understanding exactly how heavy dinosaurs were is tricky. Some people say *Spinosaurus* was the largest predator ever to walk on Earth. Others believe it was a fight between *Tyrannosaurus rex*, *Giganotosaurus* and *Spinosaurus* for that top title.

There's another question about *Spinosaurus* and that is we still don't really know what its body looked like . . . was it two-legged or four-legged? And if it was four-legged, how did it walk with such big claws? Did it walk on its knuckles or wrists or on the palms? The truth is that we just don't know. Yet.

THE SKULL

Evolution isn't a person, obviously. It's a force of nature. But if you were to imagine it as a person, then it would be an artist who 'recycled' ideas again and again, rarely creating anything new. Lots of different animals evolve similar adaptations, which allow them to do the same thing. *Spinosaurus* is a good example. Even though *Spinosaurus* and crocodiles were not closely related, their skulls looked very similar.

A lot of people say how similar *Spinosaurus* is to a crocodile. A quick look at the skulls and you could easily think they were closely related but they're not. So, why do things that aren't related look similar? The answer is that sometimes, the environment shapes evolution and we find that living in the same area or eating the same thing often makes different animals look similar. This is called convergent (*con verr-jent*) evolution. If two things 'converge', it means they come together and look or act the same.

  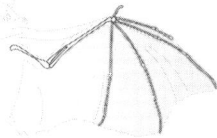

Pterodactyl   Bird   Bat

One of the best examples of this is flight. Pterosaurs flew, as birds and bats do. They all have wings, but they are not closely related. Instead, they evolved in order to be able to do the same thing – fly! Because *Spinosaurus* and crocodiles both hunt in the water, detecting and catching fish, nature has shaped their evolution similarly.

Both types of predator hunted in the water, so shared lots of details on the skull. If it works for one animal, why change it?

1. We don't have a complete *Spinosaurus* skull yet but we do have pieces. We also have a more complete skull from the closely related *Irritator* and can use it to predict things. Based on these fossils, we think the

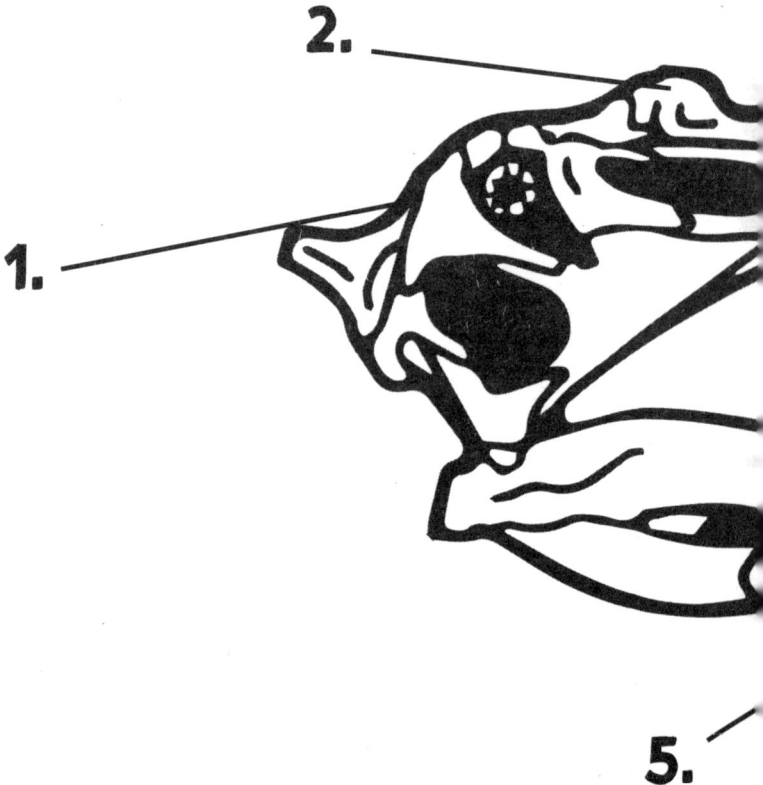

2.

1.

5.

Spinosaurus skull was about 1.75m in length. That's massive! Get someone to measure you and then see how big you would be compared to a *Spinosaurus* skull.

2. There was a small, bumpy-looking crest at the top of the snout, in front of the eyes.

3. Looking at the little pits at the end of the snout,

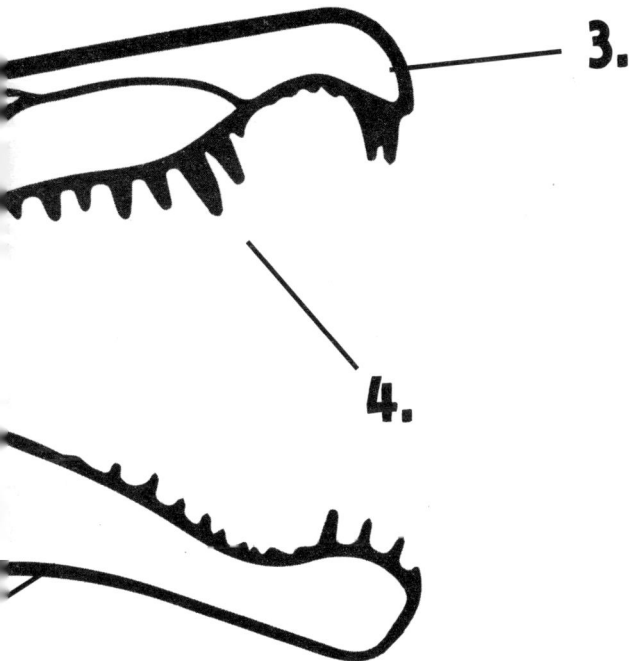

3.

4.

it appears that they are not little pits but little holes that go all the way through to the other side of the bone. Although we aren't certain, they could have been pressure sensors. We think that when *Spinosaurus* held its snout in the water, it could feel the tiny vibrations made by prey, just like crocodiles and alligators do.

4. The long skull had a narrow snout with a rounded tip, which allowed more teeth to be attached. On each side of the upper jaw, there were six or seven teeth at the end of the jaw and then another 12 on each side. The second and third teeth were much bigger, followed by smaller teeth then larger teeth again. Large teeth in the lower jaw helped fill this space, making it perfect for grabbing slippery fish.

5. When researchers studied the strengths and weaknesses in the skull of *Spinosaurus*, they found that it wasn't as strong as it might have been. They compared it to the skull of other spinosaurs, such as *Baryonyx*, and to living members of the crocodile family. Although it was a very strong skull for biting down, it couldn't twist very much. This means that *Spinosaurus* would not have eaten other dinosaurs, as they would have struggled more than fish and could have caused serious injury.

Something we can do with fossils is to run what we call isotope (*i-so toe-pp*) analysis on the bones and teeth. Isotopes are atoms that have slightly changed from their original appearance, and analysing them can tell us everything from what an animal ate or where it lived, to what the climate was like millions of years ago.

When scientists did isotope analysis on some teeth from a *Spinosaurus*, the results showed that they were semi-aquatic (and spent a lot of time in or near water). They were compared to other theropod dinosaurs such as *Carcharodontosaurus* and with turtles and crocodiles alive today. The results showed that they lived less like other dinosaurs and more like these modern aquatic reptiles.

We think that *Spinosaurus* spent time on land and in the water. It could hunt for food in both habitats and compete with other predators both in and out of the water.

THE SKELETON

1.

Spinosaurus was most famous for the huge row of spines running down its back.

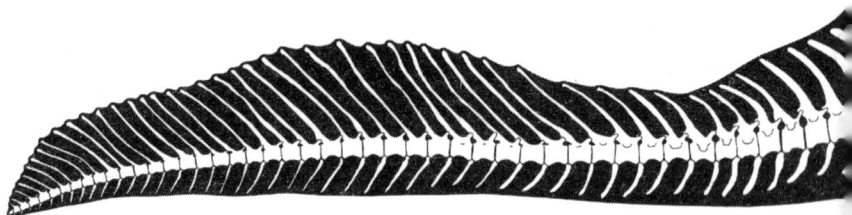

6.

Spinosaurus had back legs shorter than you would expect on a theropod dinosaur of this size.

2.

Spinosaurus had heavy, dense bones.

3.

The skull had a long and narrow snout with sharp, rounded teeth.

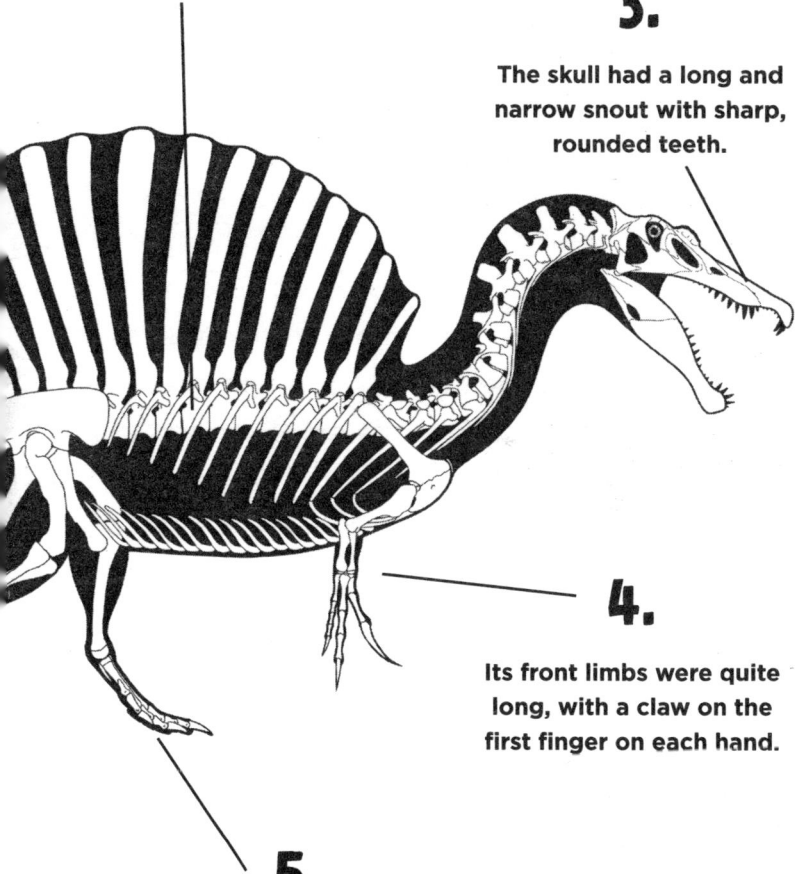

4.

Its front limbs were quite long, with a claw on the first finger on each hand.

5.

Spinosaurus had wide, flat feet with broad claws.

THE SKELETON

One of the biggest puzzles in palaeontology is the incomplete fossil record. If only part of a skeleton is found, then how is a scientist ever to understand fully what that animal was like? We can have a good idea certainly, but it will always involve guesswork (even if it's backed up by good science). It's a bit like receiving a 500-piece jigsaw as a present, but when you open the box, only 25 bits are there. Okay, you might get an idea of what the finished picture should look like but it won't be easy. This is the problem with many dinosaurs but especially with *Spinosaurus*. This predator has caused so many arguments, because we only have some of the bones. It's a theropod that is being updated all the time.

1. *Spinosaurus* **was most famous for the huge row of spines running down its back.**

These spines were really long bits of bone on the top of the vertebrae. Some of these spines could be as much as 1.65m in length. You have small spines on some of your vertebrae but they are around 2cm long – over 80 times shorter than those *Spinosaurus* spines.

2. *Spinosaurus* had heavy, dense bones.

Theropod dinosaurs had lots in common with each other. One thing they nearly all had was lightweight bones that were air-filled (like honeycomb). Animals such as *Tyrannosaurus rex* and *Allosaurus* (and even the birds alive today) had bones like this. *Spinosaurus* was different, as it had heavy, dense bones. Aquatic animals such as whales, dolphins and manatees have heavy bones too, to help make sure they don't always float to the surface. The heavy leg bones of *Spinosaurus* are a clue that it spent a lot of time in the water.

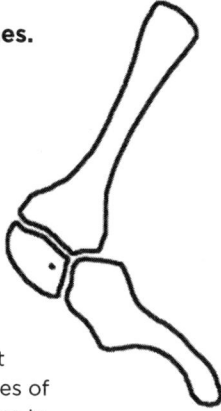

3. The skull had a long, narrow snout with long and sharp, rounded teeth.

While the rest of the body was pretty weird, the head looked like a huge crocodile skull had been stuck on top. The skull had a long, narrow snout with long and sharp, rounded teeth – perfect for catching and holding on to fast, slippery fish.

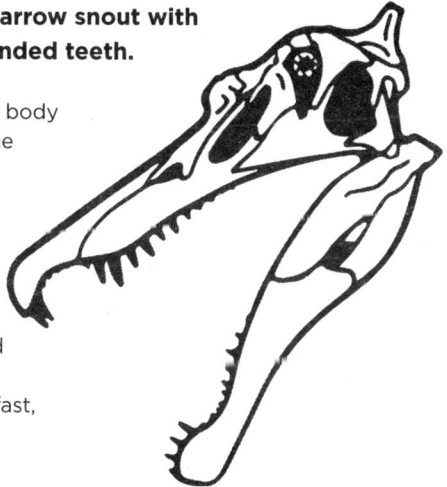

4. Its front limbs were quite long with a claw on the first finger of each hand.

While the back limbs of *Spinosaurus* were fairly short, its front limbs (the arms) were quite long. It had a large claw on the first finger on each hand. Like all theropods, *Spinosaurus* could not twist its arms and hands so that the palms faced the ground. Instead its palms would have faced each other.

5. *Spinosaurus* had wide, flat feet with broad claws.

Spinosaurus was a theropod dinosaur. Theropod means 'beast foot' and most theropods had narrow and flexible feet. *Spinosaurus*, though, had wide, flat feet with broad claws. These would have been rubbish for running and chasing prey but perfect for paddling and swimming through the water.

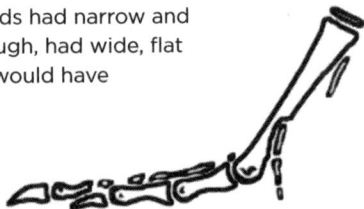

6. *Spinosaurus* had back legs shorter than you would expect on a theropod dinosaur of this size.

Whales evolved from animals that walked on land. As they evolved during their move from land to water, their legs became shorter and shorter and at some point would have been too short for walking on land. *Spinosaurus*'s shorter back legs give scientists a hint that it was an aquatic predator.

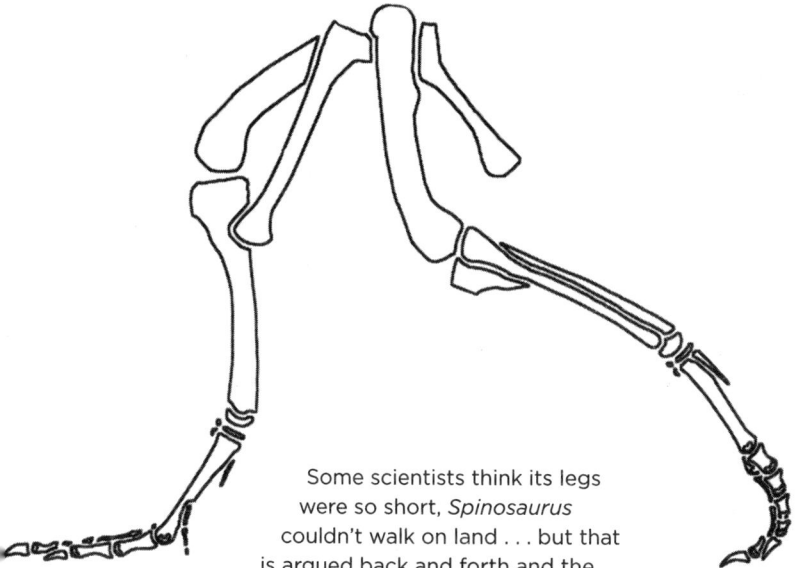

Some scientists think its legs were so short, *Spinosaurus* couldn't walk on land . . . but that is argued back and forth and the truth is that we don't know how it walked. Even though the femur (thigh bone) was short. It had a huge ridge on it, which would have allowed for lots of big muscle attachments on the tail, meaning that *Spinosaurus* may have been able to use its tail to swim, in the same way a crocodile does.

THE BODY

Imagine an animal that weighed almost as much as four big African elephants, had a head like a giant crocodile, a body like a stretched-out *T.rex* and a huge sail all the way down its back. Now imagine how it walked – did it walk on four legs to support that massive weight? Was it able to move around on its two short but strong back legs? How did it balance? Did it use its front legs for support, maybe walking on its knuckles like a gorilla or on the side of its 'hands' to take some of that massive weight? Could it even walk on land at all, or was it forced to stay in the water, only coming out to lay eggs on land once a year? The sad news is that you won't find the answers here, because there's still so much we don't know about *Spinosaurus*.

For years, we thought *Spinosaurus* was a two-legged theropod, like most of the others. That made the most sense. It almost looked as though a huge sail had been glued on to the back of a more 'standard' theropod like a *Megalosaurus*. Then, when the closely related *Baryonyx* was discovered and was found to have strong front limbs that could have allowed it to walk on all fours, we started to think that *maybe*

Spinosaurus did the same. Then some scientists thought that maybe the spines supported a big energy-storing fatty hump (like we see on camels today) and that this would mean it definitely walked on four legs.

Then it was thought to be two-legged again but would have walked with crouched legs. Now it appears that it was a long and 'stretched-out' theropod, with a long skull, a long strong tail and short legs. In this new understanding, it's still difficult to imagine how it walked. We all seem to have different opinions about *Spinosaurus* but if you ask me, I think these big predators spent most of their time in the water, where their weird bodies would have been supported and their odd shape would have allowed them to swim. I reckon they stood to hunt but the water would have helped them do this. Maybe soon we'll know for sure.

THE BODY

4.

We are still debating
what the sail was for.

3.

The tail was muscular
and powerful.

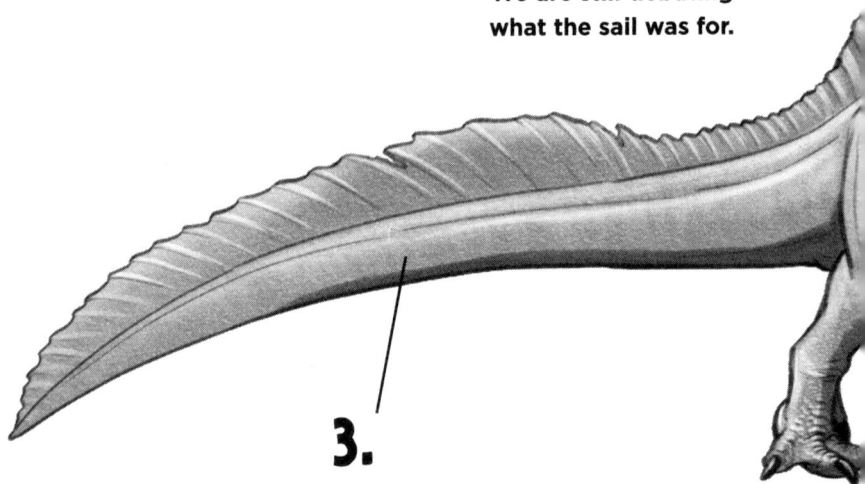

1.

It is thought that the row
of long spines on the vertebrae
were connected by skin,
making a big sail.

2.

The nostrils were high
up, near the nose.

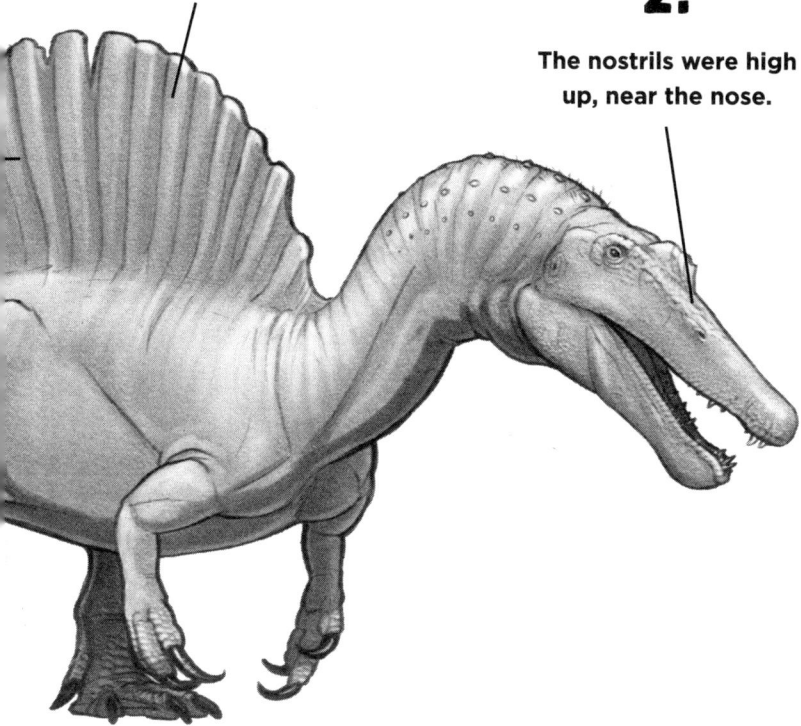

1. We call the big thing on the back of a *Spinosaurus* a sail but it may not have been. The idea is that this row of long spines on the vertebrae was connected by skin, making a very big (and awesome-looking) sail. But because palaeontologists haven't found any *Spinosaurus* skin imprint fossils yet, we can't be 100 per cent certain.

2. How often do you think about your nostrils? How often are you grateful for them? Well, *Spinosaurus* had excellent nostrils. They weren't at the end of the snout (like a crocodile) but they were high up, near the nose. This means *Spinosaurus* could have held the end of its snout underwater, with its mouth open, in order to catch fish. Because they were high up on the face, the nostrils would have acted like a snorkel, so the dinosaur could hunt and breathe at the same time.

3. The tail on a theropod dinosaur often acted as a balance for the rest of the dinosaur. Without the long and heavy tail, the animal would have been top heavy and might have toppled forwards. The tail on a *Spinosaurus*, though, had extra benefits. It looks as though the base of the tail was muscular and powerful, which would have allowed *Spinosaurus* to be a strong swimmer, using its tail to power through water.

Hunting

There is no doubt that *Spinosaurus* was a serious predator but how did it hunt? Looking at the bones and anatomy can give us clues, and different parts of the *Spinosaurus* body suggest various ways of hunting.

Here are some of the ways in which *Spinosaurus* may have hunted:

Like a crocodile in the water

It's almost impossible to look at the skull of a *Spinosaurus* and not think how similar it looks to a crocodile skull. The shape is so similar and the teeth look almost the same. It even appears to have little holes and pits in the end of the snout, which may have helped it sense vibrations and pressure changes in the water. Maybe *Spinosaurus* swam along in rivers, hunting large fish, just like a crocodile does.

Like a heron from the shore

As fish swim past, a heron stands absolutely still. Its head moves at lightning speed and splashes into the water to catch its prey. Maybe *Spinosaurus* was an ambush hunter, standing on the shore, watching the water for hours until an unsuspecting fish came by. *Spinosaurus* did have a very flexible neck, which could have allowed it to strike quickly. Maybe *Spinosaurus* stood on the riverbank in the shallow water, hunting large fish, just like a heron.

In a group like thresher sharks

It's so easy to look at a *Spinosaurus* and see all the 'big' stuff . . . the crocodile-like head, the massive claws, the weird sail . . . but the tail might also have helped with hunting. Some aquatic hunters, such as thresher sharks, use their long flexible tails to confuse and even stun prey. Maybe *Spinosaurus* used its tail to hunt and may have even hunted in groups, like thresher sharks sometimes do, to make sure their hunting is even more effective.

Spinosaurus could have hunted like a crocodile, or like a heron or like a thresher shark, or possibly like all three. We don't know, but looking at the remarkable body and anatomy of this giant aquatic predator and thinking about animals alive today may help us answer yet another *Spinosaurus* mystery.

3. It's time to talk about the sail . . . it's one of the most well-known things from any of the dinosaurs but what was it for? Remember that evolution does everything for a reason – the giraffe's long neck, the chameleon's funny eyes and the eagle's hooked talons all have a purpose. The *Spinosaurus* sail would have been the same and helped the predator in some way. There are several possible ideas:

Thermoregulation (*thur-mo reg-u-lay-shun*)

This means that the sail may have been involved in controlling the body temperature. We don't know how dinosaurs controlled their temperature. Were they warm-blooded, or endothermic (*en-doh thur-mik*) and made their own heat, like mammals and birds do? Were they cold-blooded, or ectothermic (*ek-tow thur-mik*) like reptiles and amphibians or were they somewhere between the two, like some fish such as tuna and mako sharks? Maybe *Spinosaurus* needed to warm its huge body, especially if it spent a lot of time in the water. If the sail had lots of small blood vessels under the skin,

then maybe they could have helped warm the large dinosaur – a very early form of sunbathing.

Or the sail may have been used for cooling down – using the network of blood vessels in the opposite way. Elephants use their ears like this, helping them cool down when the sun is hottest. Maybe the sail was used to cool *Spinosaurus* in the hot Cretaceous environment in North Africa.

Energy saving

Some scientists believe that the spines acted as an anchor for a large fatty hump. When there wasn't much food available (during dry seasons maybe), then a fatty hump full of energy could have kept the *Spinosaurus* alive. Although nothing has a hump quite like this nowadays, the nearest thing would be the camel's hump.

Hydrodynamic (*hi-dro di-nam-ik*) swimming

Imagine you were in control of evolution and were able to design the perfect shape for a swimming animal. You wouldn't design a swimming animal in the shape of a brick, as that would not cut through the water. Instead, you'd make it narrow and smooth, so that it could move through the water easily and quickly. If an animal can swim like this, it can be said to be hydrodynamic. Maybe the *Spinosaurus* sail helped it swim better. It does look a little bit like

the sailfish's rectangular sail, which is used to stop the big predatory fish from swinging side to side when swimming. Maybe the *Spinosaurus* sail acted in the same way and helped this giant theropod move in the water.

Display

Many animals display to each other, either to attract a mate (like peacocks) or to warn others, 'go away, this is my territory' or to scare off predators. Okay,

it's safe to say that because they were possibly the biggest land predators ever, nothing tried to eat a *Spinosaurus*. So the sail wasn't used to scare predators. It seems possible that these sails were for display. If they were to attract a mate, then we might expect the sail to be a different size in males and females (peacock tails and deer antlers are only used for display in males).

This leaves territory. If a stretch of river had more than one *Spinosaurus* hunting on it, then each would want the best place for fishing. But if they were ambush hunters, they would have needed to stay still and not move about lots, displaying. Maybe the sail was like a flag, a clear signal to others about the animal's size and strength. Almost like a fight entirely in their heads. This territory display would work if *Spinosaurus* could stand on the riverbank with its mouth in the water or if the body was in the water, with only the snout and sail above the surface. I think the sail was for displaying territorially but like so many things with *Spinosaurus*, we still don't know for certain.

CHAPTER 5

DINOSAUR DOMAINS

HABITATS AND ECOSYSTEMS

HABITATS AND ECOSYSTEMS

When *Spinosaurus* was alive (112–93.5 million years ago) during the mid-Cretaceous, some of the most well-known of all the dinosaurs were around. We know lots about different species from across North America, South America, Asia, Europe and even Antarctica. But prehistoric Africa remains a bit of a mystery. We know of a few species but not what life was like for those we *do* know about. If it wasn't *the* biggest, then *Spinosaurus* was definitely among the biggest predators in the area.

There were other large predators around at the same time but their bodies show us that they ate different things, so would probably not have competed with *Spinosaurus* for food. As well as crocodiles, fish (including sharks), turtles, lizards and plesiosaurs, some large sauropods were also found in the same area. How many of these animals opposite do you recognise?

The theropods of northern Africa all looked so different (in their bodies and skull shapes) that they would probably have taken up different positions in their ecosystems, meaning they would have eaten different things and hunted in different ways. This

Bahariasaurus

Carcharodontosaurus

Rugops

Deltadromeus

would have been a lot like life now on the African savannahs – think about leopards, lions and cheetahs. They are all related but because their bodies are different, their behaviours are different and they hunt in different ways, meaning there is less competition.

Paralititan

Aegyptosaurus

Ouranosaurus

Whereas most dinosaurs lived on dry land, it looks as though *Spinosaurus* preferred a different type of habitat and lived along the shorelines of estuaries, rivers and maybe on the seashore. It would have been found living in mangrove swamps and forests, hunting among the tall and exposed roots of trees found in areas where the tide washes over them twice a day. These very tough trees can live in water up to one hundred times saltier than most other plants. The swamps are full of fish and other animals and would have provided a brilliant breakfast buffet for a hungry *Spinosaurus*.

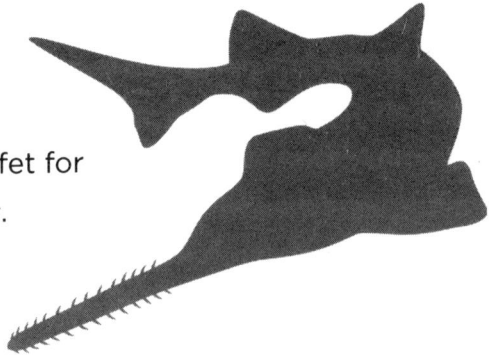

So what did the mighty *Spinosaurus* eat? We all say it ate fish (it definitely had the right adaptations on its body) but what is the evidence? Well, first there were lots of large fish in the area. Giant sawfish, huge catfish and big lungfish were found in the waters where *Spinosaurus* hunted. So, the fish were available. Also, there is

some fossil evidence. There are signs of fish scales in the fossil of a closely related *Baryonyx*, showing that some spinosaurs definitely did eat fish.

Was that all they ate? Well, it appears not. *Baryonyx* has also been found to have had the bones of a young *Iguanodon* in the area where its stomach would have been.

And a pterosaur fossil from South America has been found with a sharp spinosaur tooth stuck into it. This tells us that although the different spinosaurs did eat fish, they also ate other dinosaurs and prehistoric animals. What we don't know, however, is whether they hunted or scavenged.

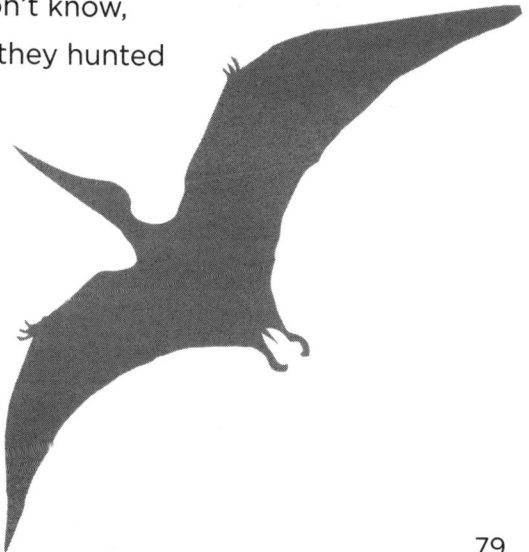

TEST YOUR DINO KNOWLEDGE HERE!

How long was a *Spinosaurus* skull?

Where have *Spinosaurus* fossils been found?

What gives scientists clues that *Spinosaurus* may have been an aquatic predator?

What sort of habitat did *Spinosaurus* live in?

What does hydrodynamic mean?

All the answers are in the text and at the back of the book.

HOW WE RECONSTRUCT AND DRAW DINOSAURS

As technology and science moves forward, our understanding of dinosaurs and other prehistoric life is improving all the time. We can now use lasers to scan fossils, we have special computer programmes to understand how prehistoric animals walked, ran or flew, and we are finding new fossils almost every day. One area of science which has really improved over the last few years is dinosaur art. How do we take information from scientific research and create awesome and accurate drawings, paintings and digital images? Well, we need a palaeo artist for that, someone who specialises in making dinosaurs as real as possible. Who better to ask than our very own Ultimate Dinosaurs palaeo artist Gabriel Ugueto. Here's how he drew *Spinosaurus*.

'Trying to reconstruct an animal that has been extinct for tens of millions of years, and one that no human has ever seen, is no easy task. Often, it takes hours of research, including reading many scientific papers, before I can even start drawing. After doing several rough sketches of *Spinosaurus* in different poses, I settled for the one opposite. In this position it shows the elongated snout, the dorsal sail along its back and its powerful hand claws.

The skeletal anatomy of some extinct animals, including that of several dinosaur species, is fairly well known, and I often start by looking at the fossilised skeleton of the subject I plan to illustrate. Unfortunately, most dinosaur skeletons are incomplete, fragmented, or crushed after millions of years of harsh geological forces. So, before I attempt to imagine how the dinosaur appeared in life, I must first reconstruct its skeleton. *Spinosaurus* is known from six incomplete specimens, so the skeletal reconstruction I created is based on pieces from all these different individuals. Often, a lot of bones are missing, so I compare them to the bones of related species. This is one tool I use to help fill the missing gaps in the fossil evidence

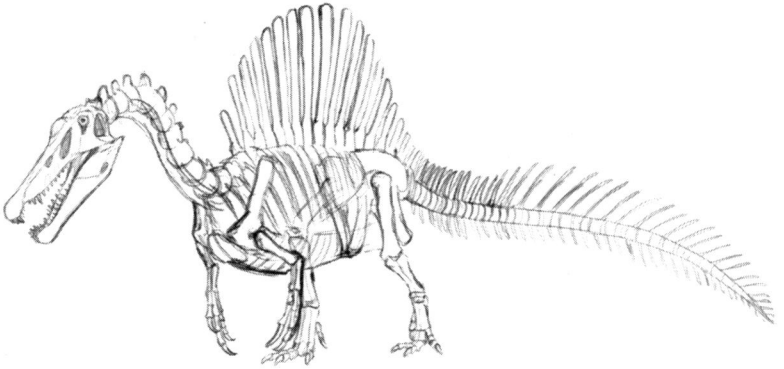

Bones can tell us a lot about the outside appearance of an animal. Although in life their shape is almost always covered by skin and muscle, bones give us clues about the size of muscles and how they were attached to the skeleton. The next step in my *Spinosaurus* reconstruction was to add muscle and fat over the skeleton frame I'd created. The shape of muscles in animals such as crocodiles and birds helped me reconstruct the overall appearance. Sometimes, even the texture of the bones can also tell us how the skin or external covering may have looked in life. For example, the fossilised arm bones of *Velociraptor* preserve a series of knobs that indicate the various points where large feathers were anchored. Similar knobs are also visible in the wing bones of modern birds.

Very rarely, soft tissue like skin, scales, or feathers fossilise as impressions. This gives a lot of extra information to the artist, like the texture of the skin or the shape of the scales. Discoveries such as these have given us a good idea of how feathers were distributed in many dinosaur species.

For me it is extremely important to have a thorough knowledge of the anatomy, general appearance and behaviour of animals alive today. Understanding the anatomy and behaviour of modern dinosaurs (today's birds) and their relatives, the crocodilians, helps me a lot when reconstructing extinct dinosaurs.

Finally, I try to find out as much as I can about what the climate was like when the animal I am reconstructing was alive, as well as the type of ecosystem in which it lived. This sort of information can help with the colour, the amount of fat, or possible display structures an extinct dinosaur may have had in life. However, it's always important to remember that there is still much we don't know when reconstructing extinct animals, meaning palaeo artists are often required to use a little guesswork.

Nothing is known about the external appearance of *Spinosaurus*. Could it have been completely covered in small scales? Or perhaps it had some areas where fine hair-like spines were present. We don't know. Based on its size, position in the dinosaur tree of life and its suggested habits, I opted to give *Spinosaurus* a scaly skin with some covering of fine spines on its neck that could be remnants from a more fuzzy ancestor.

Armed with all the tools mentioned before, paleo artists are capable of reconstructing dinosaurs with what should be a high level of accuracy, and now more than ever before, we are able to recreate dinosaurs closer to how they appeared in life. I'm so lucky to be a palaeo artist during a time when so many interesting discoveries are giving us a much clearer window into the world of dinosaurs and how they lived.'

CHAPTER 6

DODGING DINOSAURS

EVOLUTIONARY ARMS RACE

EVOLUTIONARY ARMS RACE

There are lots of things that drive evolution, making a species change over time. It could be a particular habitat, such as the cold Arctic and walruses with lots of blubber to keep them warm and sensitive whiskers to hunt in cold murky waters, or feeding techniques (just think about cobras and their excellent vision and venom-injecting fangs). There's also the competition between predator and its prey, like the cheetah with its incredible speed and the gazelle with its ability to twist and dodge when running from a predator. Sometimes what pushes evolution comes from others of your own kind. Sometimes, you need to show others just how big and how powerful you are and where your territory starts and theirs ends.

THE BATTLE

It's afternoon in the mid Cretaceous – a long, hot sunny day, just over 97 million years ago. It's Egypt but it looks very different to the way it does today. The land is criss-crossed with rivers, streams, swamps and estuaries. There are thick clumps of palm trees, standing along the edge of a very wide and very deep river. The water is slow-flowing and almost crystal clear, after being filtered through rock and sand for millions of years. Long, lush water plants sway in the current while pterosaurs glide

In evolution, there's always a reason behind an adaptation. There's nearly always an obvious reason why an animal has stripes or spines or feathers or something else. It's called **natural selection** and means that these adaptations and changes in either the body or behaviour gives the animal a better chance of surviving and having young, making sure the species continues.

But sometimes, an animal has something that looks really silly and actually increases the chances of it being caught and eaten. Seems weird, doesn't it? Why would an animal evolve something that might get it killed? Well, sometimes it shows just how strong you are and how much energy you have if you have something like this. And it means you have more chance of getting a partner and having young, because you look so impressive.

The best example is the peacock's tail. Males have a really big tail. In fact, it's so big, bright and heavy that it makes it easier for predators to catch them. But managing to survive despite this shows a future mate just how strong the male is. So, although some adaptations seem weird (or even unhelpful), there is always a reason for them.

over the river, young ones snapping at giant dragonflies. It looks so calm. But not for long.

A pair of huge jaws rush through the surface to snap at a young pterosaur that almost flew too close to the water. But the little flying predator swoops aside safely and goes in search of food somewhere less deadly. The huge jaws of a *Spinosaurus* sink beneath the surface again, a plume of spray clouding from his nostrils, making a beautiful rainbow in the sizzling heat. He dives and swims down the river in search of prey, his strong tail sweeping slowly side to side.

As he moves through the cool water, with his large sail cutting through the surface, he spies another of his kind. A female. She's much bigger than him and has a row of thick black stripes on her huge sail. She's resting in the shallows, with a dead sawfish between her jaws. The sawfish is large but appears tiny next to this giant aquatic dinosaur. She rips into the flesh with her powerful claws, before gulping down chunks of soft meat.

With the dry season this year lasting so long, food has been harder to catch and has made

the male *Spinosaurus* desperate. Usually, two giant spinosaurs like this would simply look at each other to see who was the bigger and stronger – who would win the fight. But times are tough and although she is far bigger, she also has food. The male *Spinosaurus* swims over.

She senses him before seeing him. The delicate little ripples in the water from his body are picked up by the sensors on her snout. She looks up and arches her body, giving him a full view of her sail. It's saying: 'Stay away'. But he swims closer. She drops the huge sawfish in the water and opens her mouth wide – the inside is pale and shows up brightly against her dark body. Another sign to warn him off. She doesn't want to fight him but she will if he doesn't move away . Still he creeps forward. He wants that fish. She flicks her tail to show her power, sending clouds of sand and fine mud swirling in the water. For a moment, they lose sight of each other. The male swims forwards. He reaches the fish, the smell of blood in his nostrils. He begins to tear into it, the water around him still cloudy. The big female is nowhere to be seen. Scared off, maybe.

With a terrifying rush, she slams into him, knocking him over. As he tumbles, he opens his mouth and hisses loudly, swallowing water as he does. The huge female slips back into the deep water and swims with her body arched, showing off her size and power. The male follows, ready to fight. When food is so scarce, both predators are prepared to fight to the death. The water is deep and both giants loop in wide circles, eyeing each other. He swims at her and manages to grasp her tail with his long jaws. His sharp curved claws sink into her tail too and she lashes wildly, trying to pull away. She reaches round and her claws hook onto him, tearing into his sail. Both roll, clawing and snapping their jaws. They're exhausted already and need to reach the surface to breathe. The female tries to break away to reach the surface but his claws are still in her tail and he's not letting go. With one mighty sweep of her tail, she surges up, with him close behind. Both break the surface at once, gasping for breath. Filling their lungs, the dinosaurs slip underwater once more.

Here, their sails appear to shimmer and sparkle and again, she turns her body to show that impressive sail. But he's too hungry or too stupid to heed the warning. He lunges forwards, mouth wide open. They lock jaws, sharp cone-shaped teeth cutting into each other. With their long jaws snapped shut, they push each other, wrestling to show strength now. He manages to drag his claws along her neck, cutting deeply. She's much bigger and stronger than him but he's faster, and being hungry has made him confident. As his yellow eyes flash brightly in the deep, clear water, he can almost taste the sawfish waiting for him. He uses his strong tail to swipe hard at her.

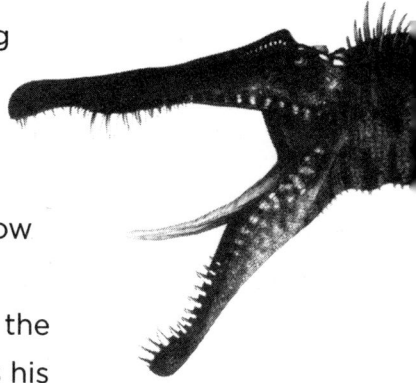

These giant fish hunters are not built to fight. They display to impress, using their sail, their powerful sweeping tail and their wide mouth. Fighting is too dangerous. They're both injured. Both are weakening. She's losing.

The huge female *Spinosaurus* can feel herself getting weaker. She hadn't eaten for weeks before the sawfish and her energy is low. She needs to escape. The smaller male loosens his grip with his mouth as he tries to reposition his deadly teeth. The massive female sees her chance and bites down hard instead. He loosens his claw and they are locked mouth to mouth. He starts to turn his body but she violently twists in the opposite direction. As her teeth are locked into the upper part of the snout, her twisting puts a huge

amount of force onto it. Although a *Spinosaurus* snout can slightly bend upwards and downwards, it can't twist at all. She continues to roll her body through the water and the pain makes him follow in the same direction but he's not quick enough and the force is too much. His upper jaw snaps off, near the nostrils.

He releases his claws and pushes back. As his snout sinks to the bottom of the riverbed, he rockets to the surface, in pain and short of breath. She follows him, ready to make the kill, but he uses his powerful tail and flexible neck to snake through the water and make a quick escape. He's alive and badly injured but he'll survive to hunt another day. He'll have to learn how to hunt again, using only his claws but he won't ignore a warning sign from a big female *Spinosaurus* next time.

Although we don't have a *Spinosaurus* fossil like this, I have seen lots of Nile crocodiles with missing upper jaws. When I used to live in a national park in Uganda, I would sometimes see crocs with these terrible injuries. I never saw a fight end in this way but I used to imagine what it would have been like. Because *Spinosaurus* was so similar to crocodiles in many ways, maybe they may have had these same fights.

FOSSIL
FINDER

Through the different 'Fossil Finder' sections in my *So You Think You Know About . . . Dinosaurs?* books, you've learned how fossils are formed, where to look for different fossils, how to stay safe when collecting and even how to take casts and use 'acid' to clean them, but then what? What do you do once you have your fossils? That's up to you. Either you can have them as a nice collection on a shelf or in a drawer just because it's cool. Or maybe you can start to collect like a real scientist and to do that, you'll need to take notes. Lots of them.

All scientists and museum curators keep detailed notes on every one of their specimens, from when and where it was found to the species identification. If you can do this, then you will be preparing yourself to be an actual scientist or museum curator. And, if you discover that one of your fossil finds is actually very important and you either loan it or give it to a museum, then you will be able to give them all this info, rather than just, 'Erm, I found it either three or six years ago and it was definitely from western Scotland. Or maybe southern England.' See how annoying that would be? And believe me, you might remember now but when you have several hundred fossils or when you're older, you will start to forget these little details.

You'll need a notepad, a pen or pencil, a compass and maybe a camera (this is a nice extra but not essential).

First of all, you need all the information (we call it 'data' in science) from where and when you found your fossil. Let's imagine you've found an ammonite and it looks like this one.

I've made a template below that you can start to use in your notebook. If you want to add bits or change stuff, that's great. Let's imagine you filling out the form after your fossil find.

Everything you collect must have a **fossil ID code** and each one should be different. You can use a system in your number to help you. Maybe it tells you the date and person who found it, as well as the number. Maybe the code for this fossil is 18BG001. This is what the code might mean. The first two numbers could stand for the year. So 18 could mean the fossil was found in 2018. The next bit of the

18BG001

Fossil ID code
Fossil species:
Found (date):
Found (location):
Formation:
For sketches:

Description:

code could be the initials of the person who found the fossil. So, BG would be me, Ben Garrod. The last three digits might show the number of fossil found in that year – 001 would tell me that this is the first fossil found in that year, 2018.

Next, when you are looking for the **fossil species**, go through books and online identification guides to help you get the right ID. Make sure your fossil species is actually found in the area you've found your fossil. For example, there won't be any *Spinosaurus* bones in the UK, no matter how hard you look and how much they look like them. Maybe it's something similar. Many species look similar, so check the small details.

The **date** is easy but important. Include the full details. Next, the **location**. Imagine you've found your ammonite on the north eastern coast of the UK. Where exactly though? Can you narrow it down? Well, you can say the nearest town or village. Let's imagine it's the seaside town of Whitby (famous for its Jurassic fossils).

The next bit is slightly more tricky but will test your skills as a young scientist. What is the **formation** like? Is it Jurassic or Cretaceous, for example? Is it limestone or mudstone, maybe? You'll have to do some research but this will really help your understanding of your collection.

Finally, make some **sketches**. You might not be very artistic but that doesn't matter. You just need to look at the details and copy them. If you find an ammonite, don't be tempted to draw something like this:

This sort of drawing doesn't tell you much. It sort of looks like a snail or an ammonite. Look more closely at your find. Does it have lumps and bumps? Are the little ridges close together or far apart? Make sure you label your drawing with size and colour.

Then maybe draw the area where you found the fossil. Was it near rocks or in the water? A quick sketch can help you find more in the future.

Fossil ID code	18BG001
Fossil species	Androgynoceras
Found (date)	2nd January 2018
Found (location)	Whitby, UK
Formation	Jurassic Mudstone

By taking detailed notes like these each time, your collection will be much more scientifically important and useful.

QUIZ ANSWERS

PAGE 38

Who was the first person to identify an ichthyosaur skeleton?
Mary Anning.

Which word is Richard Owen famous for making up?
Dinosaur.

When was *Spinosaurus* alive?
Mid Cretaceous 112–93.5 million years ago.

Which modern reptile does *Spinosaurus* look similar to?
Crocodile.

What special discoveries have scientists made from *Ichthyoventor* fossils?
It had two sails running down its back.

How long was a *Spinosaurus* skull?
1.75m.

Where have *Spinosaurus* fossils been found?
North Africa – Egypt and Morocco.

What gives scientists clues that *Spinosaurus* may have been an aquatic predator?
Short back legs for a theropod of its size, muscular tail for swimming, wide flat feet for paddling.

What sort of habitat did *Spinosaurus* live in?
Rivers and estuaries, mangrove swamps.

What does hydrodynamic mean?
Shaped to swim quickly and easily.

How many did you get?

Jog your memory here

GLOSSARY

Adaptation This is a change in an animal, caused by evolution. An adaptation can be a change in the body (such as stripes on a zebra or wings on a bird) or it can be a behaviour (such as wolves hunting in packs and fish swimming in shoals). An adaptation helps an animal or species survive.

Aquatic Means to do with the water. An aquatic animal is one that lives in the water, like a fish. If something is semi-aquatic, then the animal spends some time in the water and some time on the land. A crocodile is semi-aquatic.

Convergent evolution This is where two things that are not very closely related evolve to have a similar adaptation. The best examples of this are the wings of birds, bats and pterosaurs. These animals are not very closely related but have all evolved wings because they're the best things to allow an animal to fly.

Divergent evolution This is where several closely related species (that all share something in common) start to change, so that they can live in different habitats or move or hunt in different ways. A good example of this is mammal limbs. All are closely related but the original mammal limb (with five digits) has changed and now there are bat wings, horse hooves, whale flippers and your own hands. They all look so different but all evolved from the same thing.

Ectothermic This means 'cold blooded' but it's a rubbish term, really. The animal still has warm blood but it means the animal warms its body up from the outside environment. A snake is ectothermic, using the sun to warm its body up for energy.

Endothermic This means 'warm blooded' – also a rubbish term. Because ecothermic animals also have 'warm' blood, it doesn't tell us much. Really, being endothermic means you can make your own heat inside your body. All mammals, for example, are endothermic.

Geologist A scientist who specialises in geology.

Geology This is the science that looks at the Earth and how it works. It especially examines the different types of rocks that are found in different parts of the world and what they can tell us.

Isotope There is lots that can be said about isotopes. It's a bit complicated and you need to understand some chemistry and physics to really appreciate them. Basically, isotopes are elements that have been changed slightly from what they originally were. For example, not all hydrogen atoms are the same. There are different types of hydrogen, with different numbers of neutrons. These are tiny particles that don't have an electrical charge. So, there is hydrogen-1, hydrogen-2, and hydrogen-3. Some of these break down faster than others and can be used by palaeontologists not only to look at the age of fossils but also to see where they lived and even what they ate.

Vertebrae These are the backbones in an animal. Lots of vertebrae make the spine. A single one is a vertebra.

ULTIMATE DINOSAURS
BEN GARROD

TYRANNOSAURUS REX

SPINOSAURUS

OUT NOW

DIPLODOCUS

ANKYLOSAURUS

VELOCIRATPTOR

OUT IN SEPTEMBER

STEGOSAURUS

MICRORAPTOR

TRICERATOPS

COLLECT THEM ALL!